AFRICAN AMERICAN
MUSICIANS &
ENTERTAINERS

AFRICAN AMERICAN
MUSICIANS &
ENTERTAINERS

EDITED BY JOANNE RANDOLPH

Enslow Publishing
101 W. 23rd Street
Suite 240
New York, NY 10011
USA

enslow.com

PIONEERING
AFRICAN
AMERICANS

Library of Congress Cataloging-in-Publication Date

Names: Randolph, Joanne, editor.
Title: African American musicians & entertainers / edited by Joanne Randolph.
Description: New York, NY : Enslow Publishing, 2018. | Series: Pioneering African Americans | Includes bibliographical references and index. | Audience: Grades 5-8.
Identifiers: LCCN 2017020672| ISBN 9780766092501 (library bound) | ISBN 9780766093911 (pbk.) | ISBN 9780766093928 (6 pack)
Subjects: LCSH: African American musicians—Biography—Juvenile literature. | African American entertainers—Biography—Juvenile literature.
Classification: LCC ML3929 .A37 2018 | DDC 780.89/96073—dc23
LC record available at https://lccn.loc.gov/2017020672

Printed in the United States of America

To Our Readers: We have done our best to make sure all website addresses in this book were active and appropriate when we went to press. However, the author and the publisher have no control over and assume no liability for the material available on those websites or on any websites they may link to. Any comments or suggestions can be sent by email to customerservice@enslow.com.

Photos Credits: Cover, p. 3 David Redfern/Redferns/Getty Images; p. 7 Alexander Alland, Sr./Corbis Historical/Getty Images; p. 8 Alfred Eisenstaedt/The LIFE Picture Collection/Getty Images; pp. 10, 11 Library of Congress Prints and Photographs Division; p. 13 Gilles Petard/Redferns/Getty Images; p. 15 Michael Ochs Archives/Getty Images; p. 18 Pictorial Press Ltd/Alamy Stock Photo; p. 19 Hulton Archive/Getty Images; p. 21 F Burke/The Sydney Morning Herald/Fairfax Media/Getty Images; pp. 22, 23, 29, 41 Bettmann/Getty Images; p. 27 Museum of Science and Industry, Chicago/Archive Photos/Getty Images; p. 32 Gaston Paris/Roger Viollet/Getty Images; p. 35 John Springer Collection/Corbis Historical/Getty Images; p. 36 Smith Collection/Gado/Archive Photos/Getty Images; p. 38 George Karger/The LIFE Images Collection/Getty Images; p. 39 John D. Kisch/Separate Cinema Archive/Moviepix/Getty Images; interior pages newyear/Shutterstock.com (curtains), nata415/Shutterstock.com (music notes).

Article Credits: Diane Bailey, "Mississippi Music," *Appleseeds*; Kathiann M. Kowalski, "Spiritual Songs in Code," *Cobblestone*; Geeta Dardick, "Born to Sing the Blues," *Cobblestone*; Art Tipaldi, "B.B King & Lucille," *Footsteps*; Ruth Tenzer Feldman, "'Music's My Language,'" *Cobblestone*; Hugh McCarten, "A Synthesis of Sound," *Cobblestone*; Darienne Oaks, "Swing It: The Story of Peg Leg Bates," *Cricket*; Diana Childress, "Josephine Baker's Two Loves," *Cobblestone*; Clayton Robinson, "The American Negro Theater," *Footsteps*; Judith M. Williams, "Abram Hill," *Footsteps*; Lisa Clayton Robinson, "Frederick O'Neal," *Footsteps*; Vicki Hambleton, "Sidney Poitier," *Footsteps*; Judith M. Williams, "Wild About Harry," *Footsteps*.

All articles © by Carus Publishing Company. Reproduced with permission.

All Cricket Media material is copyrighted by Carus Publishing Company, d/b/a Cricket Media, and/or various authors and illustrators. Any commercial use or distribution of material without permission is strictly prohibited. Please visit http://www.cricketmedia.com/info/licensing2 for licensing and http://www.cricketmedia.com for subscriptions.

CONTENTS

CHAPTER ONE

MISSISSIPPI MUSIC

The sayings "having the blues" and "jazzing things up" come from music. The music called the blues was born from the suffering of slaves. Jazz can be flashy and full of surprises. Blues and jazz don't sound alike, but they have something in common: the Mississippi River.

But why the Mississippi? Why not the mountains in Colorado or the deserts in Arizona? The reason starts with the river itself.

RHYTHM OF THE RIVER

In the late 1800s, by the Mississippi around Memphis, Tennessee, black laborers—many of whom were former slaves—were hard at work clearing the river's delta for farming. Men and women who had worked together as slaves were again working side by side. The work was backbreaking, but singing eased the burden. For one thing, the tempo helped everyone keep pace. Workers who sang together found it easier to work together, "One-two-three-PULL," "one-two-three-DIG." The rhythm of music matched the rhythm of work. And the feeling of the music matched the feeling of the work.

African American workers load cotton and other cargo at a dock in Memphis.

As it is today, singing then was also an effective way to express feelings: sadness and frustration, hope and longing. Through words and music, difficult work became a little less terrible. The rhythms and words were a combination of African songs, church hymns, and work chants. Eventually, they blended together to become the Delta Blues.

This photograph shows a group of African American musicians playing along the Mississippi River in 1937.

Upriver in St. Louis, Missouri, another kind of music was becoming popular: ragtime. Known for its syncopation, ragtime was great dance music. African American composer Scott Joplin became known as the King of Ragtime.

THE BIRTH OF JAZZ

As the Mississippi River flowed, so did the music—downstream, to New Orleans, Louisiana. New Orleans had a mixed population of blacks, whites, and immigrants, and it had one of the world's busiest ports. Just about everyone in the city made a living from the river. As different people worked side by side, their music began swirling together like the water and mud of the Mississippi itself. The fast rhythm of African chants greeted the trained ear of classical European music. The harmonies of church spirituals added their voices, and once in a while some mischievous ragtime syncopation would slide in. The amazing sound of jazz was born.

The river carried cotton and other goods, but it carried culture, too. There's a song whose lyrics say, "Jazz came up the river from New Orleans/Looking for a better-paying job it seems." Thousands of people traveled the Mississippi, many going north to find a better life, and others just for fun. Many travelers cruised the Mississippi on showboats featuring everything from minstrel shows to brass bands.

Riverboats also stopped at smaller ports in the countryside, where farmers could listen to the music. They went home, played these new sounds on their homemade instruments, and gave the music their own twist. The Mississippi River had another new kind of music: bluegrass.

Steamboats carried people and freight up and down the Mississippi River. This illustration shows two boats traveling from New Orleans to St. Louis in 1870.

Everywhere along the Mississippi, musicians met, and played, and sang, and then traveled on. But they hummed as they left, taking the music with them to wherever the river led next.

Pioneering African American musicians and entertainers changed the shape of American music and added bright swathes of color to the culture of entertainment in the United States.

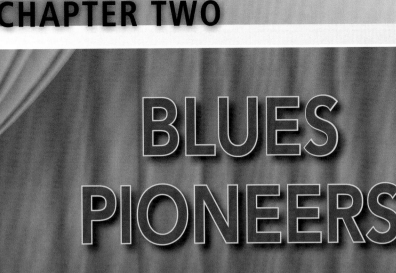

CHAPTER TWO

BLUES PIONEERS

Blues music had its roots in slavery. Most slaveholders did not allow their slaves to read or write. Many slave owners also banned the playing of drums, which they were afraid would beat out coded messages among slaves. Slaves even were restricted from talking to one another during work. But singing spirituals seemed harmless to their masters—especially if the songs had themes related to the white owners' Christian religion.

African American spirituals usually were about struggles. Many tunes offered hope for freedom; some even included coded details on how to get to a place of liberty. "Steal Away to Jesus" describes being called by the Lord. But the song also encouraged slaves to sneak away for secret meetings. There were other codes embedded

Singing helped the time pass as African Americans worked in the fields.

in the music as well. Not only did the songs give the enslaved blacks an outlet for their feelings, but they also gave them hope for a better future.

Besides spurring on slaves with the hope of freedom, these songs have played a central role in American music. Gospel, jazz, blues, rock, and rap music all can trace their roots back to the great folk tradition of spirituals.

As blues developed at the end of the nineteenth century, it took elements from the spirituals as well as work calls and chants. Blues music is characterized by the call-and-response format and its "blue," or flat, sad-sounding notes.

BORN TO SING THE BLUES

People say that Bessie Smith was born to sing the blues. Her life began in poverty in 1895 in Chattanooga, Tennessee. Her father died when she was a baby, and her mother died when she was nine. Often she and her brothers and sisters were hungry. From an early age, she understood the meaning of "feeling blue."

As a young girl, Bessie sang the blues in the streets of Chattanooga to earn money for food and clothing. One day Ma Rainey, the most famous blues singer of the time, passed by and was impressed by the quality of Bessie's voice. She helped and encouraged Bessie with her singing.

When Bessie was seventeen, she was singing in Selma, Alabama, one night when a white man named Frank Walker heard her perform. Walker loved the hardness of Bessie's voice. He was over-whelmed by her soulful rendering of the blues.

During the 1920s, Bessie Smith—the Empress of Blues—rose to the top. She recorded 180 songs and sold more records for Columbia than any other black star. She also sang in theaters and nightclubs across

Standing five feet ten inches tall and weighing 210 pounds, Bessie Smith's imposing appearance reflected her powerful voice.

the country. She sang to packed houses in Philadelphia, Detroit, and Chicago. She wore glamorous satin gowns with fancy furs and feathers. There is no doubt that Bessie Smith was the finest blues singer of her time—perhaps all time. Her style influenced all of the female jazz vocalists that followed her.

Despite her talent and popularity, however, Smith's success was short-lived. At the height of her career, she took to drinking gin and squandering her money. At the same time, the country entered a depression, which meant that people had little money to spend on such luxuries as records. In addition to all this, public interest in Smith's style of singing began to wane. With the invention of the microphone, audiences began to prefer a softer, sweeter sound. Smith tried to adapt her singing to the new style, but she was unsuccessful. Her record sales fell, and she was no longer booked into the top clubs. The Empress of the Blues had lost her throne.

Even in death, Smith's story reflected the blues that she sang. The year was 1937, and it looked as though she might have been making a comeback. Her drinking was under control, and she was on a singing tour in the South. She was about to return north for her first recording session since 1933. But her hopes and dreams were shattered when the car she was in was hit by a truck on a Mississippi highway. She lost too much blood and died in the hospital.

Bessie Smith made a million dollars during the height of her career, yet she died penniless. She was buried in Philadelphia. The epitaph on her tombstone reads, "The Greatest Blues Singer in the World Will Never Stop Singing, Bessie Smith, 1895–1937."

B. B. KING AND LUCILLE

Blues musician B. B. King performed on stages around the world, making more than fifteen thousand appearances with "Lucille," his famous guitar.

Riley B. King was born September 16, 1925, on a plantation near Indianola, Mississippi. As a teen in the 1940s, he performed in a local gospel choir. But when he discovered he could make money

B. B. King hard at work at a recording studio in 1963. King had many replicas made of his special guitar.

playing blues on his hometown streets, he decided to make this style of music his focus. King was influenced by guitarists such as Blind Lemon Jefferson, Lonnie Johnson, and T-Bone Walker.

While living in Memphis, Tennessee, in the late 1940s, King performed in clubs on the Tennessee side and the Arkansas side of the Mississippi River. One night, King was playing at an Arkansas juke when a fight broke out between two men vying for a woman's attention. As they fought, they spilled a trash can filled with burning kerosene, and flames quickly engulfed the dry, wooden walls and floor of the juke. Everyone escaped, but King remembered that his black Gibson guitar was still inside and ran back into the burning building to save it. When he learned that the woman involved in the fight was named Lucille, he decided to name his guitar after her.

King became a traveling performer after his song "Three O'Clock Blues" was a hit in 1951. After his most famous song, "The Thrill Is Gone," was released in 1969, King became the nation's most successful blues artist. He continued to be a successful artist for many decades before his death in May 2015 in Las Vegas, Nevada. He was buried in Indianola, Mississippi.

CHAPTER THREE

JAZZ GREATS

Jazz is a uniquely American form of music that has been constantly developing since its emergence in the early years of the twentieth century. Jazz has roots in both Africa and Europe, tracing its beginnings to blues and ragtime. Simple but powerful, the blues managed to convey both sorrow and resilience in the face of adversity.

Ragtime, which captured the country's imagination in the 1890s, combined aspects of both black and white musical traditions. Played on a variety of instruments and even sung, ragtime achieved its widest popularity as music written for the piano. On a typical tune or "rag," a ragtime piano player's left hand played a steady one-two marchlike rhythm; his right hand played a melody slightly ahead of or behind the beat, creating an exciting effect called syncopation. The pulse of this music was ragged rather than smooth, hence the name "ragtime."

The earliest jazz bands probably developed out of the New Orleans brass bands that played at parades, dances, and funerals around the turn of the century. Ensembles like those led by early

Freddie Keppard plays a cornet, which is similar to a trumpet.

trumpet giants Buddy Bolden (1877–1931) and Freddie Keppard (1890–1933) combined the soul and spirit of the blues with the rhythmic jolt of ragtime and created a brand-new kind of music. It would come to be called "jass," and soon thereafter, "jazz."

New Orleans jazz (which was springing up in other parts of the country, too) featured a basic jazz concept—improvisation—in its lively arrangements of marches, blues, rags, and popular songs. In a New Orleans band, the musicians improvised together, in an ensemble style. This spontaneous, do-or-die element lent jazz a thrilling quality, especially in contrast to the sedate music of the day.

During the early twenties, as jazz spread north to St. Louis, Chicago, and New York City, the best players introduced the next important trend—the "hot" soloist, such as New Orleans soprano saxophonist Sidney Bechet (1897–1959).

But the most acclaimed of these new performers was another New Orleans musician, trumpeter Louis Armstrong. Nicknamed "Satchmo," Armstrong was a matchless singer and natural showman, and he soloed with an impassioned intensity unrivaled in jazz.

Louis Armstrong

"MUSIC'S MY LANGUAGE"

Louis Armstrong was born on August 4, 1901, in New Orleans, Louisiana. While still a teenager, Louis Armstrong was befriended by Joe Oliver, the "king" of jazz trumpeters, and his career as a musician took off. He played on riverboats with Fate Marable's band and performed with Kid Ory's band when "King" Oliver left it to establish his own band in Chicago. In 1922, Armstrong joined Oliver's Creole Jazz Band, with whom he made his earliest records. Armstrong played second cornet to Oliver, backing him up during his improvised "breaks." The two became a sensation.

Armstrong left King Oliver's band in 1924 to join Fletcher Henderson's band for its opening in New York City. Duke Ellington noted, "When [Henderson's] band hit town and Louis Armstrong was with him, the guys never heard anything like it. There weren't enough words coined for describing that kick."

In the mid-1920s, Armstrong returned to Chicago, where he organized the Hot Five, then the Hot Seven, and the Savoy Ballroom Five to make his own recordings on the Okeh label. With musical hits such as "Muskrat Ramble," "West End Blues," and "Heebie Jeebies," he began to achieve worldwide fame as a jazz trumpeter and singer.

Armstrong followed King Oliver's advice to play the theme, or "lead line," straight, but he also created a new style. He was a genius at using the broad range of "expressions" on a cornet or trumpet, although Armstrong rarely played the cornet after 1928. With his pure tones, high notes, and clear phrasing, Armstrong gave his horn a voicelike quality. He also used his gravelly speaking voice as if it were an instrument, and he was one of the first jazz performers to "scat" (sing without words). Armstrong summed up this blend of voice and instrument in explaining why he never encountered communication problems on his tours abroad: "Music's my language."

Through the mid-1940s, he often led swing bands of his own. After World War II, the big band sound became less popular, and bebop and rhythm and blues were on the rise. Neither style interested

Louis Armstrong and his band play in Sydney, Australia, in 1954.

Armstrong, but big bands were expensive to maintain. In 1947, thanks to a renewed interest in traditional jazz, Armstrong brought together the All Stars, a small combo that he led until his death in 1971.

Throughout his life, Armstrong performed with the best jazz musicians, composers, and singers. Among them were Benny Goodman, Duke Ellington, Billie Holiday, Sidney Bechet, Ella Fitzgerald, and Bessie Smith. Armstrong not only established many of today's jazz improvisation techniques, but he also made this uniquely American music accessible to every American.

A SYNTHESIS OF SOUND

Among many other talented individual players were a group of New York–based pianists who made up the Eastern "stride" school. They included James P. Johnson, Thomas "Fats" Waller, and Willie "The Lion" Smith, and they made jazz rhythmically freer by jumping ("striding") their left hands in wide arcs up and down the bass end of the piano. Johnson in particular had an important influence on the young Duke Ellington, who has been more of a catalyst for the evolutionary changes in jazz music than perhaps any other jazz musician.

When Ellington and his band established themselves in New York City in 1923, they were playing dance music (mostly popular tunes) with a slight jazz tinge. But Ellington was drawn to the sounds of authentic jazz. He sensed that there was a way to integrate the rough style of New Orleans jazz and the new "hot" solo styles with something musically broader and more sophisticated. With this in mind, Ellington began adding distinctive individual "voices" to the band.

Duke Ellington (1899–1974) was one of the most influential jazz musicians in history.

Ellington is shown here with his band in 1931. Ellington did not like to refer to his music as "jazz." He called it the more general "American music" instead.

The first of these was trumpeter James "Bubber" Miley. Then Ellington set about finding fresh approaches to orchestration that would highlight the soloists against a background of other instruments. Finally, Ellington began writing the compositions that would win him an immediate nationwide audience and endure to become the backbone of the standard jazz repertory of today.

Gradually, Ellington's band grew to twelve pieces. (Later it would include as many as eighteen.) Each new arrival provided a new voice for Ellington's tonal palette. Ellington, unlike other bandleaders, did not make his musicians conform to a group style. Instead, he showcased their particular talents, and the result was a unique instrumental blend.

The Ellington orchestra's triumphant four-year engagement at Harlem's Cotton Club (1927–1931) became a turning point.

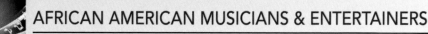

Ellington's synthesis of sound gave jazz a vibrant, urban edge that it would never lose. Ellington's genius also proved that jazz could be more than just entertainment, and for the first time, the music was recognized as an art form to be taken seriously.

In the mid-1930s, a new jazz craze known as swing music, with a compelling, highly danceable rhythm, swept the nation. Although clarinetist Benny Goodman (1909–1986) was proclaimed its king, the music actually had its roots in Fletcher Henderson's and Ellington's orchestras of the 1920s. By the end of World War II, swing had given way to another jazz innovation called bebop. Popularized by Dizzy Gillespie (1917–1993) and Charlie "Yardbird" Parker (1920–1955), bebop expanded jazz's harmonic, rhythmic, and tonal possibilities, building on the foundation Ellington had helped lay. As jazz continued its evolution into the fifties, sixties, and beyond, Ellington kept current but never changed his basic approach. For each new generation of listeners, Ellington's timeless music is the vital link between early and modern jazz styles, from Louis Armstrong to Wynton Marsalis (1961–). Today, nearly twenty years after his death, Ellington still towers over the jazz world, and he is considered by some to be the greatest composer that America has yet produced.

CHAPTER FOUR

DAZZLING DANCERS

With the rising popularity of jazz, ragtime, and other forms of music, so too was there a rise in dancing and other forms of entertainment. African Americans led the way, pioneering new styles of dance, such as tap, swing, and even modern dance.

THE STORY OF PEG LEG BATES

If Mother Bates ever found out that her son was dancing in the streets, she would "wup" him good, but five-year-old Clayton couldn't help himself. His feet needed to dance as surely as his heart needed to beat. While waiting for his next shoeshine customer, Clayton rhythmically snapped his white polishing rag in the air, joyfully stomping around to its catchy beat. People walking by sometimes dropped a few coins in his shoeshine kit to show their appreciation. Clayton sure didn't tell his momma about that either!

The money Clayton earned shining shoes was needed at home. His father had deserted the family when Clayton was three. Mother

Bates struggled to make ends meet while raising Clayton by herself and caring for her own mother. A strong woman, she labored from "kin work" to "kant work"—which was often more than from sunup to sundown—as a sharecropper in the cotton and corn fields near Fountain Inn, South Carolina. On Sundays she worshiped at the Baptist church in town, making Clayton come along, too. Clayton deeply loved his mother and tried to respect her wishes, but her church taught that dancing was sinful, and dancing was something he just couldn't keep himself from doing.

When Clayton was twelve years old, he knew it was time to offer his aging mother more help. He'd heard there was work at the cottonseed gin, a factory where machines removed cottonseeds from the fibers, then crushed them to extract their valuable oil. At first Clayton's mother refused to give him permission to work near such dangerous machinery. But Clayton hated sharecropping and, like a small child pleading for a puppy, constantly begged his mother to change her mind. Worn down by weeks of pleading, Mother Bates finally told Clayton she would take the matter up in prayer with the Lord. The next morning, she informed her son that he had God's blessing to take the job.

At the cottonseed gin, several buildings were connected by an auger conveyer, a long trough with a corkscrew-shaped blade along the bottom. The blade turned night and day, pushing cottonseeds in the trough from one building to another. Clayton was still getting used to the layout of the factory when, around three o'clock one morning, a light went out in the back of one of the buildings. Not quite knowing what to do, Clayton went to investigate. As he crept cautiously across the floor in the darkness, groping his way through the unfamiliar rooms, he suddenly felt his left foot step into air and slip down into the auger conveyer. The sharp blade, twisting like a screw, ripped through his flesh and began to devour his leg. Intense pain exploded through Clayton's body. His piercing screams reached the only other person working that night. He found Clayton, stopped the machinery, then ran to get help.

Clayton was carried home to his horrified mother, and doctors came to examine his injury. His leg was so terribly mangled that they had no choice but to amputate. They cut off Clayton's left leg below the knee as the boy lay across his kitchen table. In those days, "colored" people just weren't sent to hospitals.

This is a cotton gin from the 1920s. It is a complicated machine with many moving parts that can pose a danger to anyone working with it.

It took Clayton more than a year to recover from his surgery. He learned to walk with crutches and then on a crude wooden leg that his uncle whittled for him. In time, Clayton taught himself to do everything the other kids at school could do, from baseball, to gymnastics, to horseback riding. Although the mill owner bought him a peg leg to replace the homemade leg, Clayton vowed he would never return to the mill.

Determined that the loss of his leg would not stop him from doing whatever he wanted to do, Clayton experimented with dancing while wearing only one tap shoe, on his good leg. Tapping with his good foot, he would work the bottom of his peg leg to create unique sounds and rhythms. Having a peg leg added an interesting dimension to his dancing, he discovered. At fifteen he began entering amateur dance contests. The audiences loved his dancing, and with his glowing grin and sparkling deep brown eyes, he won first prize in every contest he entered.

Clayton made up his mind to become the best tap dancer around. He had never taken a lesson in his life, but he watched the two-legged tap dancers and copied their steps. For hours every day, Clayton made up rhythms in his head and worked them out with his foot and peg leg until they sounded right. Combining gymnastic leaps with his dancing, he created an electrifyingly flashy step he called the "jet plane." After a running start, he would jump high into the air, do a split with his legs, then land on the tip of his peg, with his good leg stretched out behind him and his arms wide open as if he were soaring. He finished his routine by hopping backward on his peg leg all the way offstage.

To earn money, Clayton would hobo the local trains to dance on the streets in nearby towns. He danced alone, swinging away

A true performer, Clayton Bates did not let the loss of his leg stop him from dancing. In fact, he became a unique and skilled dancer.

without any music, his peg leg providing a driving rhythm. But dancing in the streets was a very hard and lonely way to make a living. When he felt his routine was as polished and flashy as he could make it, Clayton decided to hobo the trains up the East Coast, dancing at each stop on his way to New York City, the dance capital of the country.

In the 1920s, theaters in New York were racially segregated. Clayton performed in black theaters on the vaudeville circuit, as well as in the segregated theaters that were only for white people. Although blacks were not allowed in these theaters, white performers would blacken their faces with burnt cork to entertain the white audiences by impersonating the singing and dancing of African Americans. Never allowing physical or racial barriers to get in his way, Clayton also performed "black-faced" in the early part of his career so the white audiences wouldn't know he was really a black man. As his popularity grew, Clayton stopped rubbing his face with the burnt cork and became Peg Leg Bates, the legendary black one-legged, tap-dancing man!

Bates began to dance with other well-known black entertainers, including the famous Bill Bojangles, with whom he toured Europe, creating a clever three-legged tapping routine that thrilled audiences in Paris. A very dapper dresser, Bates had fifteen peg legs made to match his suits. Audiences found his act so stupefying that they would leap to their feet, whistling and shouting "MORE! MORE!" He entertained the king and queen of England, performed with the great Louis Armstrong, toured with the Harlem Globetrotters basketball team, and danced at Radio City Music Hall in New York City. He was the first African American to perform on *The Ed Sullivan Show*, one of the most popular television shows of the

1950s and 1960s, on which he appeared an astonishing twenty-two times. During the Korean War in the early 1950s, Bates spent a lot of time visiting and performing for wounded soldiers who had lost legs or arms. When he tapped for young children in the New York State schools, he told them, "Remember, you can do anything you want to, providing you want to bad enough."

Bates danced for fifty-two years, right into his sixties. He died in 1998, at the age of ninety-one, convinced that losing his leg was God's way of giving him his character and a unique dancing style. Peg Leg Bates danced with a beaming smile, sharing his unwavering determination with people of all ages, colors, and cultures.

JOSEPHINE BAKER'S TWO LOVES

Nineteen-year-old Josephine Baker did not plan to become an expatriate when she signed a contract to dance in an African American show in Europe in 1925. But she fell in love with Paris. The "City of Light" had glamour and sophistication, and its racial tolerance amazed her. She could try on clothes in elegant department stores and be served politely in cafès. Asked about her most vivid memory of her opening night, she recalled the banquet afterward: "For the first time in my life, I was invited to sit at a table and eat with white people."

In St. Louis, where Baker was born in 1906 and had grown up, segregation was so strict that laundries run by African Americans advertised, "We only wash white people's clothing." In 1917 she and her brother Richard had watched the city burn during a race riot. How could she return there? Besides, Paris loved beautiful,

31

Josephine Baker was known for her uninhibited style of dance. When she died in 1975, she was buried with military honors due to her service for France during World War II.

daring "La Baker." She danced, acted in plays and films, and began a singing career. "J'ai deux amours" became her theme song. "I have two loves," it went, "my country and Paris."

When she finally came back to New York in 1935 to star in the Ziegfeld Follies, the St. Moritz Hotel refused her a room. She longed for "my France and my freedom."

In 1937 Baker became a French citizen. During World War II, she joined the French Resistance and won many medals for bravery.

Baker remained in France after the war but fought for civil rights in the United States. She refused to perform for segregated audiences on her concert tours and spoke at the March on Washington in 1963. To show that interracial harmony was possible, she adopted children from many different countries.

Baker died in Paris in 1975, where she was starring in a show about her life and still singing about her two loves—"my country and Paris."

CHAPTER FIVE

THE AMERICAN NEGRO THEATRE

The American Negro Theatre (ANT) was the most famous and influential black theater company of the 1940s. Actors Ruby Dee, Harry Belafonte, and Sidney Poitier and acclaimed playwright and novelist Alice Childress are just a few of the hundreds of artists who were part of the company early in their careers.

They were all drawn to ANT for its innovative attitude and its range of opportunities for black actors, writers, and crew members. ANT was founded in Harlem in 1940 by playwright Abram Hill and actor Frederick O'Neal. For some time, Harlem had been a thriving site for African American drama with theaters such as the Lafayette and the Harlem Experimental Theatre and with the black theater company known as the Krigwa Players. During the Great Depression, just before ANT was founded, the Harlem site of the government's Federal Theatre Project had employed local artists as playwrights, directors, technicians, crew members, and actors.

ANT helped fill the gap created when the Federal Theatre Project ended and left many African American actors and crew members looking for new positions. Abram Hill and Frederick O'Neal wanted to make space for as many talented people as possible, and they wanted to do this in a new way. For them, traditional theaters often encouraged a "star system." This meant that actors were considered most important. It also meant that there was fierce competition among black actors for the limited roles available.

Hill's and O'Neal's intention was to create a theater that would work as a cooperative. They envisioned a place where actors, directors, writers, and crew members would be equally important and where all members would share the expenses and profits. Hill and O'Neal sent postcards to other black actors, writers, and technicians explaining their idea and inviting them to join them. Then, in June 1940, they officially founded the American Negro Theatre with a group of eighteen artists.

The group chose its name partly for its acronym. Members liked the abbreviation ANT because they felt it symbolized that all involved in this theater would work together just as ants do. The company agreed to become a financial cooperative, and the members agreed that anytime they performed outside ANT, they would give ANT 2 percent of the payment they received—

Ruby Dee (1922–2014) is probably most famous for her role in the play and film *A Raisin in the Sun*.

another sign of the members' commitment to the theater. ANT eventually established its theater in the basement of the 135th Street branch of the New York Public Library, a space that fit 125 people.

ANTs first production was *On Striver's Row*, written by Abram Hill. It was a satire about residents of Harlem's Striver's Row, a neighborhood full of middle-class black families who were always "striving" for even higher social status. It ran for five months, was well-attended, and received good reviews. *On Striver's Row* became Hill's most popular play, and it solidified the American Negro Theatre as an important Harlem institution, eventually producing nineteen plays, including twelve original productions. Although ANT was not segregated, it focused on plays that reflected Harlem.

In 1944, ANT produced the play that would become its breakout hit: *Anna Lucasta*. An immediate success, *Anna Lucasta* moved to Broadway after just five weeks, and its popularity continued

Ernestine Rose (*bottom left*), the librarian at the 135th Street branch of the New York Public Library, helped build a rich collection of books, manuscripts, and art that showcased African American history and culture.

there. Only a few of the original ANT actors were chosen to be in the Broadway production. As a result, ANT actors now became restless as they hoped for their own big breaks.

Soon, ANT felt obligated to stop producing plays by local playwrights as it had been doing and produce plays by established writers that would have better chances of becoming hits.

Over the next several years, ANT did send three more plays to Broadway, but none became the hit *Anna Lucasta* had been. As the months passed, many ANT members began to feel that it was no longer enough to be just part of a "community" theater and were less excited about remaining with the company. At the same time, Harlem residents and artists no longer thought of ANT as just "their" theater and did not attend productions as frequently.

In 1945, ANT became the first black theater company to produce a weekly radio series, but the radio series' success came as the theater was beginning to decline. By the early 1950s, ANT had stopped producing new shows. During the decade in which it did flourish, ANT gave several hundred black writers, actors, technicians, and directors an opportunity to get their starts or display their talents. In some ways its end was related to its success: ANT gave many of its members the opportunity to have their work seen on Broadway or by larger audiences than they otherwise would have had. ANT also gave audiences in Harlem and across America the opportunity to see just how richly talented these artists were.

ABRAM HILL

Born in Atlanta, Georgia, Abram Hill came to New York in 1923 at the age of thirteen. He pursued his studies at City College

This is a scene from the 1945 production of *Anna Lucasta* by ANT, starring Hilda Simms (*center*) in the title role.

and received a degree from Lincoln University in Pennsylvania. He got his start in theater by working as a writer in the Federal Theatre Project.

In June 1940, Hill was one of the principal founders of the American Negro Theatre and served as executive director for much of his tenure there. Hill also wrote *Walk Hard*, *Hell's Half Acre*, and *Liberty Deferred* and was the principal adaptor of ANT's version of Philip Yordan's *Anna Lucasta*. Hill left ANT in 1948.

From 1951 to 1955, he was part of the drama department at Lincoln University. He returned to New York City in 1957, where he taught English until he retired in 1980. Hill died in New York of emphysema on October 6, 1986, at the age of seventy-six.

FREDERICK O'NEAL

An actor, director, lecturer, and administrator, Frederick O'Neal made his first professional appearance on stage in St. Louis, Missouri, on October 27, 1927, at the

Frederick O'Neal, here in 1958, acted in both stage and screen versions of *Anna Lucasta*.

age of twenty-one. He played Silvius in a production of Shakespeare's *As You Like It*. A founder of ANT, he also appeared in several of its productions.

In 1944, O'Neal played Frank when the play *Anna Lucasta* first appeared on Broadway and won both the Clarence Derwent Award and the New York Drama Critics' Award for the best supporting performance of the season. Many other roles followed, and so, too, did awards. O'Neal performed both on stage and on screen.

In the early 1960s, he accepted a visiting professorship at Southern Illinois University and another at Clark College in Atlanta, Georgia. Active in both drama and civic organizations, O'Neal received several honorary doctoral degrees—the first in 1966 from Columbia College in Chicago. He died August 25, 1992, in New York City.

SIDNEY POITIER

More than any other actor of his generation, Sidney Poitier stands out as a supreme talent to audiences everywhere. Poitier's career has lasted more than fifty years. He was the first African American to win the Academy Award for best actor, for his role in the movie *Lilies of the Field*. He has acted in and directed more than fifty movies. In 1967, at the height of his success, Poitier made more money than any other film star in Hollywood, black or white.

His career as an actor, however, came about almost by accident. He discovered acting as a young man newly moved to New York City. Born in Miami, Poitier spent his youth in the Bahamas. His family was poor, and as a young boy, he often got into trouble. At age thirteen,

Sidney Poitier is an actor, director, author, and diplomat. He has won many awards for his work.

he dropped out of school. When he was caught stealing corn and sent to jail, his father decided that his son needed a better life and sent him to live with his older brother in Miami. But Poitier had other ideas. His goal was to move to New York's Harlem, and he did so at age sixteen, full of hopes and dreams but little else. In his autobiography he recalls how devastating his first winter in New York was. Weather in his native Bahamas was never so cold.

Poitier worked at various low-paying jobs and even spent some time in the army. In his second year in New York, when he again went looking through the help wanted ads for a job, an "Actors Wanted" listing caught his eye. Poitier reasoned that acting would be easier than washing dishes. In his book *The Measure of a Man*, he wrote, "I figured that I could do the work. Acting didn't sound any more difficult than washing dishes or parking cars."

He presented himself at the American Negro Theatre (ANT) and was immediately given an audition. But Poitier, who could barely read and still had a heavy Bahamian accent, was not very impressive. He was told, "Get a job you can handle."

Poitier wanted to prove to them that there was more to him than washing dishes. So he worked to improve his reading and his English and then returned to ANT to try again. This time he was accepted as a student. Then, in 1946, he got his break in the Broadway play *Lysistrata* when a fellow student, none other than Harry Belafonte, could not perform one night. Poitier took over and, although the play was terrible, he received rave reviews.

His career would take him away from the New York theater for nearly ten years, as his fame in America and Europe grew and he concentrated on films. When he did return to the stage, it was in the play *A Raisin in the Sun,* in which he created the role of Walter Lee Younger. He writes about the play in his autobiography, *This Life:* "I knew for certain that I was meant to be an actor when the curtain came down on opening night . . . After all the doubts that had accumulated since that serendipitous meeting with the gentleman at the American Negro Theater . . . that night I was an actor."

WILD ABOUT HARRY

When eighteen-year-old Harry Belafonte walked into a Harlem theater on 135th Street in December 1945, he found an obsession that would haunt him for the rest of his life. The young Belafonte had been working as the assistant maintenance man in an uptown building and had been rewarded with two tickets to the theater by a grateful tenant.

The ANT soon found use for him as a stagehand. Eventually, his physical grace and good looks attracted the attention of Osceola Archer, the then director of ANT's Studio Theatre. She offered him a small part in Frank Gabrielson's *Days of Our Youth*. Although rough and untrained, Belafonte had a strong, almost magical presence that Archer called "electricity and tremendous appeal." Other roles soon followed.

Belafonte was not content simply to exhibit a natural appeal but wanted training in the craft. He took advantage of the GI Bill to enroll in acting classes with Erwin Piscator at the New School for Social Research in Greenwich Village. In a class with Marlon Brando, Tony Curtis, and Sidney Poitier, he was hardly a standout, yet he worked diligently.

Belafonte continued to appear in productions with ANT while attempting to pursue more lucrative employment in downtown and Broadway theaters. To earn money to support himself and his wife, who was expecting their first child, Belafonte found a position in the garment district. One evening (before working even his first day at that job), he entered a nightclub called the Royal Roost on "Cinderella Night," when amateurs were encouraged to perform. When Belafonte took the stage to sing, the audience saw the same magic he had displayed as an actor. This appearance led to a twenty-week paid singing position at the Roost.

Despite his initial success, Belafonte quickly grew frustrated with his pop singer role and refashioned himself as a folk singer.

While probably best known as a singer, Harry Belafonte began his career as an entertainer on the stage with ANT.

He sang Caribbean songs such as "Matilda," "Jamaica Farewell," and the ever-popular "Banana Boat Song," often known by its refrain "Day-o." His album *Calypso*, released in 1956, was the first album to sell more than a million copies and remained on the popular music charts more than thirty weeks.

Belafonte's fame as a singer gave him entry into Hollywood. In 1953 he made his film debut in *Bright Road*. Soon after, he appeared in *Carmen Jones* in 1954 and *Island in the Sun* in 1957. In 1959 he starred in two films, *The World, the Flesh, and the Devil* and *Odds Against Tomorrow*. The latter was notable because Belafonte, wary of the box that Hollywood created for black actors, had formed his own production company, Harbel, and *Odds* was its first film. Through the 1960s, he continued to perform as a singer.

In 1970, Belafonte returned to film, starring with Zero Mostel in Harbel's production of *The Angel Levine*. Then, in 1972, he starred in *Buck and the Preacher* with Sidney Poitier and Bill Cosby. This was a successful, lighthearted comic film that was followed by a sequel, *Uptown Saturday Night*, in 1974.

It would be twenty years before Belafonte appeared in another film, this time with John Travolta in *White Man's Burden*. The following year he played Seldom Seen, a 1940s gangster, in Roger Altman's *Kansas City*. Many critics called this performance the best of Belafonte's film career. In the role of the cruel gangster, Belafonte was finally able to relax and allow the magnetism that escaped so easily from him on the stage to finally show on screen.

Belafonte has had a long career as a performer, more singer than actor, and an even more rewarding one as an activist. He worked for civil rights in the 1960s, in the early days of the movement, and once said, "We're in a struggle for the soul of this country. We're in a struggle for America's moral center."

Through the years, as a promoter of social justice, he has rejected roles that created success for others, formed his own production company to create more positive images of blacks, and fought for causes in which he believed. His charisma, natural ability, and hard work have allowed him to overcome each setback, and he has pursued success on his own terms. He epitomizes the pioneering spirit that characterizes so many of the African American musicians and entertainers who left their marks on America's cultural landscape.

GLOSSARY

audition To try out for a part in a play or performance.

evolution The process of changing over time.

hobo To live or travel in the manner of a hobo, or homeless person; a migrant worker.

improvise To create on-the-spot variations over a basic musical structure.

juke Also called a juke joint, a tiny club in a town or in the woods in the rural South where black workers often gathered on Saturday nights to socialize, gamble, dance, and listen to the blues.

segregated Separated based on race, gender, religion, or other differences.

signature Something that acts as an identifying characteristic.

social justice Justice, or fairness, in terms of access to wealth, privilege, or opportunities and resources.

soloist A singer or musician who performs alone.

spiritual A religious folksong of African American origin.

syncopation The changing of the rhythm to stress the weaker beat, giving the music a certain unexpected, off-beat quality.

synthesis The combination of ideas to create something new.

vaudeville A type of entertainment that was popular in the early twentieth century and that featured a mix of acts, such as comedy, singing, and dancing.

BOOKS

Caravantes, Peggy. *The Many Faces of Josephine Baker: Dancer, Singer, Activist, Spy.* Chicago, IL: Chicago Review Press, 2017.

Dahl, Eric. *B. B. King's Lucille and the Loves Before Her.* Minneapolis, MN: Blue Book Publications, 2013.

Old, Wendie C. *The Life of Louis Armstrong: King of Jazz.* Berkeley Heights, NJ: Enslow Publishers, 2014.

Rohan, Rebecca. *Duke Ellington.* New York, NY: Cavendish Square Publishing, 2016.

WEBSITES

BlackPast.org

www.blackpast.org

An online guide to African American history, including "101 African American Firsts," primary documents, major speeches, and historical timelines.

Scholastic, History of Jazz

teacher.scholastic.com/activities/bhistory/history_of_jazz.htm

A brief overview of the history of jazz and the people who were well-known pioneers in the genre.

INDEX